Copyright © Gary Bentley
The right of Gary Bentley to be identified as author of
him in accordance with the copyright, Design

All rights reserved. No part of this publication may be reproduced, stored in a retrieval system, or transmitted, in any form or by any means, electronic, mechanical, photocopying, recording or otherwise, without the prior permission in writing from the author.

Unless otherwise stated, Scripture quotations taken from THE HOLY BIBLE, NEW INTERNATIONAL VERSION® NIV® Copyright © 1973 1978 1984 by International Bible Society. Used by permission of Hodder and Stoughton Limited.

Publisher: Independent Publishing Network.
First published: 2021
ISBN: 978-1-80049-299-8

Distributed by: Inspire Publications, Leeds, England
All distribution and general enquires to: garybentley@hotmail.com

Special thanks to
Kate Slater
Joe Kapolyo
Graham Brownlee

Front/back cover photograph by Adam Kontor from Pexels
Cover design by Gary Bentley
Page design by Isaac Bentley

Printed in the UK by Solopress
www.solopress.com

DAY 1: THE THRONE OF GRACE

Let us then approach the throne of grace with confidence, so that we may receive mercy and find grace to help us in our time of need. **Hebrews 4:16**

Context
The writer of Hebrews tells us that we have a great High Priest; Jesus our forerunner, tempted in every way, yet without sin. He shows us that it is possible to persevere through the darkest of times, remain faithful and stay completely on mission. He understands the extent of the emotional and physical pain of living in this world, as well as the fickle rejection and cruelty at the hands of others. Yet through it all, He kept in close relationship with Father God and had an attitude of love and forgiveness, even whilst nailed to the cross.

Today's Message
When we go through a time of difficultly, whether it's financial, illness, recovering from an injury, struggling with difficult relationships, experiencing doubt, failure or rejection. We either try to deal with it ourselves (in our own strength) or we pray and ask God to change the situation instantly, so we don't have to endure it. Although the Lord can and sometimes does do this, today's verse challenges us to consider where we instinctively turn when we enter a difficult time. Do we look inward to our own resources; become angry towards others; throw the 'faith' towel in and threaten God that we will walk away; apply emotional pressure to those around us to solve the issue, or do we approach the throne of grace?

Notice that it is not described as a throne of removing problems; a throne of wrath on those who hurt us; or a throne of vindication that proves we were right all along. These are desires that are rooted in pride, that we must bring to the throne of grace. Where we turn in times of need directly reflects where we put our trust. We are right to look to God to change the situation, but wrong if we demand revenge on others. Romans 12:19 exhorts us to not seek revenge but leave room for God's perfect judgement. It is often not the situation that defeats us, but the attitude we have.

When we pray and ask God to change a situation, He often uses it to change us. The Lord, it would seem, is less interested in the external factors, than He is about the attitudes and hang-ups of His children. He knows how much we need His grace (free and unmerited favour) and mercy (undeserved forgiveness) particularly when our responses are not as Christ-like as they ought to be. When we recognise our inability to change a situation, the quicker we let go of pride and come to His throne of grace. It is then that we are empowered to cope in situations where others give up and know joy when others only experience anger. The Christ-like recognise the opportunity in the storm for testimony to bring glory to God's faithfulness and never-ending love. Let me encourage you to come to the throne of grace in prayer. It will transform your perspective; share the burden and give you less broken relationships along the way.

Prayer
Lord, I am sorry for my pride and for expecting You to jump to my demands. Thank You for allowing me to approach Your throne of grace. I recognise that I need You more than I could ever realise. Transform me from the inside out, to be more like Jesus and bring glory to You.

DAY 2: REJECTING THE FRUIT

**But the fruit of the Spirit is love, joy, peace, patience, kindness, goodness, faithfulness, gentleness, self-control. Against such things there is no law.
Galatians 5:22-23**

Context
From verse 16 in Galatians 5, Paul talks about the difference between walking in the Spirit and in the flesh (selfish living). From verse 19 Paul lists some of the things that are evidence of living for yourself: idolatry, hatred and selfish ambition etc. He then goes on to list the fruit, or evidence, that someone organically produces when they are walking in, or led by, the Spirit. It should be noted that the 'fruit' of the Spirit and 'gifts' of the Spirit (1 Corinthians 12:1-11) are different. Jesus helps us to identify what is happening in a person by the fruit they produce:

    Matthew 3:8-10 Describes us as trees that bear good or bad fruit.
    Matthew 7:16-20 By their fruit you will recognise them.

Today's Message
During a time of worship, my attention was drawn to a basket of plastic fruit sitting on the table at the front of the church. It was there to remind us of the word God gave about it being a year of extreme fruitfulness. As I looked at the basket of fruit, the silliest thought passed through my mind, "I don't like some of those fruit, I would pick some, but not others". Instantly God said, "It is the same with My fruit. My people pick some and reject others because of their experience". It breaks God's heart when people reject certain fruit that come from walking with the Spirit. What should be organic, turns into an internal resistance, as they struggle to let someone, even God, love them, because of fear of being let down and hurt again. Or refuse to receive His joy because they would rather wear the scars of hurt like medals, holding onto anger and bitterness. Or reject His kindness because they think "why should I be kind, no one has been kind to me". What a terrible place for us to be in. Rejecting the fruit of the Spirit in our lives because we refuse to give the fear or hurt to God. To reject certain fruit is to say to the Holy Spirit, You can come to here but no further. To reject the free gift of the fruit of the Spirit, to some extent is to reject the Giver! Thereby, limiting what we can know of the character of God in our lives.

I know it's scary and makes you feel vulnerable, but you must give Him the pain you have been protecting for so long, even if the wounds feel as painful today as the day it happened. The surgeon can only make you well if you allow him to perform the operation. It's when we give the Holy Spirit full access to all areas that we begin an exchange that allows His healing process to begin. What He removes, He replaces with love, joy, peace, patience, kindness, goodness, faithfulness, gentleness, self-control. It may be a process over time, but the process will be worth it. Let Him have it all, so that you can enjoy a deep healing, evidenced by the fruit you produce.

Prayer
Lord God, the hurt still feels very raw today, and I am exhausted from carrying it and trying to hold my life together to look good on the surface. You ask for all of me, so I surrender it into Your hands. Begin an exchange of healing that produces all the fruit of the Spirit to glorify You.

DAY 3: ROOTED

A good tree cannot bear bad fruit, and a bad tree cannot bear good fruit. Every tree that does not bear good fruit is cut down and thrown into the fire. Thus, by their fruit you will recognise them. Matthew 7:18-20

Context
What we are rooted in, is where we draw our influences from for our pleasure, confidence and advice. Jesus was right there in the thick of things by day, but was never influenced by those around Him. He could spend time speaking with the adulterous woman, touch the man with leprosy and 'tango' with the Pharisees and yet remain completely uninfluenced. Because Jesus was unquestionably rooted in Father God in Heaven, He knew His identity, His authority and the source of His power. He had the backing of the whole of heaven. That's why He could go where the 'sinners' were and give of Himself and never need to seek affirmation or advice from anyone. He was securely rooted in Father God, the source of all His strength, out of which came good fruit of the Spirit, which we are still tasting to this day.

Today's Message
What, or who, you are rooted in determines the fruit you produce in your life. Good or bad. For anyone who cannot tell their trees apart, the real evidence is in the fruit. There are other indicators as to what type of tree it is: the shape of the leaves, the bark, the size etc. But this passage tells us that it might look like a good tree, but the fruit is what gives it away. The evidence of whether a tree is healthy or sick, good or bad, is in the fruit. We might look and sound like a good Christian, but it is really the fruit that reveals what we are rooted in and drawing from. Do all your roots draw on God, or do some of them reach elsewhere? Do you draw from other places for strength and guidance, such as self-help books, friends' opinions, TV shows, business leaders' mantras or even ideologies from other religions?

If we are firmly rooted in God, we will inevitably produce good fruit, the fruit of the Spirit, fruit that brings life. But if we are also rooted in other influences, we are going to be drawing on a range of mixed messages, not all of which are healthy for our spirit. This is a breeding ground for confusion and uncertainty. I am not saying we should not listen to, watch or read anything other than the Bible. Remember Jesus mixed with all kinds of people, but he did not allow Himself to be influenced by the menu of opinions.

Jesus said in Matthew 26:41, "Watch and pray so that you will not fall into temptation. The spirit is willing, but the body is weak." By being rooted in God alone, we draw on His Spirit to produce only good fruit. Do not put your roots down into anything other than God. Then you can go places and meet people, and be the influencer, not the influenced.

Prayer
Lord, if I am rooted in anything or anyone other than You, it is poisoning me. Give me the strength to place all my trust and confidence in You alone, so that my life produces only good fruit; fruit of Your Spirit working in me, that glorifies You.

DAY 4: CONFIDENCE TO ASK

Great crowds came to Him, bringing the lame, the blind, the crippled, the mute and many others, and laid them at His feet; and He healed them. Matthew 15:30

Context

I was leading a prayer meeting a few years ago with a small group of believers. An elderly lady asked for prayer because her hearing was going. Two of the ladies prayed a prayer that I have heard so many times before. You'll know what I mean. You may have even prayed it yourself when we are unsure if God will heal or not. It goes something like 'Dear Lord, comfort Claire as she visits the hospital.' I don't know if I offended anyone, but I asked the two of them to pray again, but this time for Claire's healing, which they did. The following Monday Claire reported that during the week she could hear a ticking sound in her home, but couldn't work out where it was coming from, until she realised it was the clock ticking in her hallway. She hadn't heard the clock for so long, she had forgotten it even ticked at all.

Today's Message

I am aware that many believers in faith have asked Jesus for healing and haven't received it, yet. Please don't feel condemned, I believe this is an issue far bigger than any individual; it is a false doctrine that has subverted the Church for many years into having a 'plan-B faith' that says, "The Apostle Paul described himself as having 'a thorn in his flesh' (2 Corinthians 12:7), therefore it must be God's will that I too am not healed" or "God is teaching me something or using me to reach others like me." Undoubtedly, God can turn any situation into an opportunity to display His glory. But the danger is that we accept our condition with a range of human explanations. If I were a crippled beggar in Jesus' day, yes God could use me to sit with the beggars and talk about faith, but if I were healed, I could walk to the beggars as an irrefutable demonstration of the power of God. Whether Jesus healed everyone else in the vicinity, for example, when Jesus heals the lame man in John 5:1-15, Scripture does not say. But what it does make clear is that there was not one occasion where Jesus turned someone away who needed healing. Each person who reached out to Jesus in faith received their healing without exception. If it were God's will that some should remain sick and Jesus healed them anyway, it would mean Jesus stepped out of His Father's will, acting on His own and sinned with the best intention. I don't think so! Healing is God's will.

If I went to my doctor's surgery and they would not prescribe anything because they were afraid it might not work; I would stay sick. That is exactly what is happening in our churches when we opt to play safe in our prayers of impotent religious nicety. And when those prayers don't work, we get away with saying sickness is God's will rather than acknowledge our lack of expectancy for God to heal. This fear of giving people false hope, gives them no hope at all, leaving Christ's Church powerless. This reduces the gospel to our limited experience, rather than raising our expectation to equal that which we see in the gospels and Acts. Do you share the same stirring in your spirit for God's healing power to be manifest in this world? There is still an opportunity for a miracle. We should not give up asking. What do you have the confidence to ask of God?

Prayer

Lord, You are the God that heals. I pray that I will see the wonders of God in my generation, that far exceed my limited experience. Stir a desperate faith within me to pray for the sick and see many healed in Jesus' name. Use your servant as an instrument for Your glory.

DAY 5: THE VALLEY

He restores my soul; He guides me in the paths of righteousness for His name's sake. Even though I walk through the valley of the shadow of death, I will fear no evil; for You are with me; Your rod and Your staff, they comfort me. Psalm 23:3-4

Context
When I was sixteen, I had a dream. I was standing in a field of soft green grass, young trees dotted about and gentle hills in the distance. It was a green pasture; a place you felt at peace, calm and settled. Left of where I was stood was the mouth of a valley. To the right of that, another valley. As I looked, an angel; short and wearing a grey suit, stood to my right and said, "Which valley will you choose? God wants you to take the one on the left." Immediately I responded without hesitation, "I'll take the one on the left." As I set off down the valley, everything started out fine. Then to my right, warriors began to run at me, running down the steep valley side, carrying staffs. As they attacked, I just seemed to be able to brush the attackers away, as if they were vapour. The enemy upped their attack by rolling huge boulders down the valley side. As each one became dangerously close, I found myself standing by a thick solid stone wall that spanned the width of the valley floor. As each boulder arrived, all I had to do was crouch next to the wall and the boulders would roll along the top of the wall and away. Eventually, the attack stopped when I reached the end of the valley. As I stood there, the angel appeared by my side again and said, "If you go the way God wants you to, He will protect you."

Today's Message
The warriors came from the side of the valley that meant they could have just as easily have attacked me in the other valley; had I had taken that option. No matter which valley I chose I would have had a battle on my hands. The difference is that in the left valley I did not have to do the fighting. The key was I had to be obedient to God's will, continue to move forward and use the resources that God gave me along the way. Whereas the valley on the right would have potentially destroyed me no matter how hard I fought.

Life is full of choices, sometimes extremely difficult ones. As Psalm 37:23-24 says, 'If the LORD delights in a man's way, He makes his steps firm; though he stumble, he will not fall, for the LORD upholds him with His hand.' You may have made some bad decisions and stumbled along the way, but you can never be so far from God that He cannot save you from yourself. You may not be able to change the mess from previous decisions, but you can, as verse 5 of the same Psalm says, 'Commit your way to the Lord'. It is not too late. One path says 'yes' to God, and the other leads to chaos and destruction. Both are not easy, they each have their battles to enter, but one sees the Lord fight on our behalf.

Prayer
Lord, I cannot see the outcome of the decisions I have ahead of me, but I can see the mess of previous decisions made without You. So, I commit my way to You and say yes to Your leading. Make Your way clear to me so I can know Your will and see You fight on my behalf.

DAY 6: THE SOIL OF THE HEART

"A farmer went out to sow his seed. As he was scattering the seed, some fell along the path... rocky places... among thorns... good soil." Matthew 13:3-23

Context
The farmer (God) sows the seed, which is the message of the kingdom. Interestingly, the seed is sown regardless of the condition of the heart of the receiver. That is our responsibility. We must play our part in this exchange, after all, God does not need the word, He is the Word. Therefore, it is for us, and if it's for us, it's important that we receive the message. We can see from today's reading that God scatters the seeds of the kingdom in abundance, it's not just for the theologians. The receiving of the message isn't an intellectual process. The seed is destined for the heart, not the head, the very core of our being, the engine room of our motivation, our passion and our creativity.

Today's Message
What prevents the seed of God's message flourishing in our lives?
1. Lack of depth of understanding of the received word. When the message reaches our hard hearts, we don't seek revelation that would enable it to impact our lives. So, it is left exposed for Satan to steal. Perhaps that's why we forget what we read so quickly?
2. 'No root in himself'. In other words, relying on other people's faith, ministry or support. When the difficulties come, reliance in anyone or anything other than God exposes how deep our faith and trust in Him really is.
3. More concerned about the temporary, rather than the eternal. The physical rather than the spiritual. Pleasing self, rather than God.

This leaves us unguarded to attack from three enemies:
1. Satan: when we don't seek revelation from the Holy Spirit and leave the message dangerously open to false interpretation, that could be twisted to manipulate people.
2. Tribulation and persecution: when we lack roots in God, and give up too easily.
3. Cares of this world and the deceitfulness of riches: when our reliance is misplaced.

What can we do?
1. Whenever we hear the message, pull it down deep into our hearts, meditate on it, and ask the Holy Spirit to give us revelation that activates the seed to produce life.
2. Like Jesus, establish our roots in Father God. Not relying on the faith of others to carry us.
3. Walk by faith, not by sight (2 Corinthians 5:7). Cast your cares on the LORD, and He will sustain you; He shall never let the righteous fall (Psalm 55:22).

Prayer
Lord, I love the message of the Kingdom, but I must confess that it hasn't always found good soil. Transform my heart that I might receive Your word, understand what You are saying to me, and act on it by faith. I know I have an enemy, but often my biggest battles are internal. Help me to have the strength I need to overcome, remain rooted in You and not be distracted.

DAY 7: CAPTIVATE, CULTIVATE, ELEVATE

"Still other seed fell on good soil, where it produced a crop – a hundred, sixty or thirty times what was sown." But the one who received seed that fell on good ground is the man who hears the word and understands it. He produces a crop, yielding a hundred, sixty or thirty times what was sown." Matthew 13:8,23

Context
It is one thing to hear the word, it's quite another to understand it. In the passage we read yesterday, there is no mention of intellect. The seed (the word) is something we receive into our hearts (v19), not our minds. Salvation is not gained by graduating an 'introduction to Christianity' course, and faith is not achieved through knowledge. 'Faith comes by hearing the message, and the message is heard through the word of Christ' (Romans 10:17). A divine exchange of repentance for salvation. A work of the Holy Spirit that cannot be replicated or manufactured.

Today's Message
Captivate, Cultivate and Elevate. There is a process God takes us on before He elevates us:

1. He draws us close to Him, captivating our hearts to cause us to fall in love with Him all over again, to be in awe of who He is by giving us a word that excites our spirit.
2. It is in our Father's arms where we feel the safest, but it is also where He cultivates our hearts by turning over the soil, revealing the stones, the hard places, and exposing the roots of the weeds and thorns of those things that entangle us. This is also known as the 'refiner's fire'. The painful process that brings the impurities to the surface, so that they can be skimmed off and thrown away. Isaiah 48:10, Zechariah 13:9 and 1 Peter 1:7. These things can be revealed in several ways: bad attitude; over reaction to a comment or situation; a time of immense difficulty; or temptation.
3. It is in the place of surrender and repentance where His word can establish roots and multiply to an extent far beyond our expectation. When we have hearts that are more able/willing/ready to let God get rid of the rubbish and shape us to be more Christ-like, He knows He has someone who will not be tripped up by those things and will be faithful and trustworthy to be elevated to another level. There are no short cuts in the process, and neither is it about promotion as the world understands it. It is about becoming more effective for the kingdom and leaving a legacy that says, "God was here!" That is how one simple word from God can have such a life changing impact.

Let's look at the situation from another perspective: God knows when we are heading into an unforeseen storm that would ordinarily knock the stuffing out of us. So, He steps in ahead of it and captivates us with a word, designed to be so powerful, it sees us through the impending storm, which God then uses to cultivate us by exposing and removing the rubbish. What has God said to you recently? Hold on to it and meditate on. Recognise that it might be your captivating word to see you through the storm, preparing you for a bigger arena. What is the condition of your heart?

Prayer
Lord God, captivate my heart with a word to see me through the storm. I know the cultivating is for my good and Your glory. Prepare me to take on the bigger giants and succeed in the larger arenas. I give You full access to all areas of my life and trust You.

DAY 8: TEMPLE DISRUPTION

But when the chief priests and the teachers of the law saw the wonderful things He did, and the children shouting in the temple area, "Hosanna to the Son of David!" they were indignant. Matthew 21:15

Context
Jesus entered the temple area and drove out all who were buying and selling there. He overturned the tables of the money changers and the benches of those selling (v12). The blind and the lame came to Him in the temple, and He healed them (v14).
Jesus speaks of His Father's house, "It is written," He said to them, "'My house will be called a house of prayer,' but you are making it a 'den of robbers'." (v13).

Today's Message
Have you ever experienced a work of God in your life or across your church, but certain church members object on the grounds that it upsets the tradition? Or you have been told your praise is disrupting the orderly format of the service? Or you are a troublemaker because you challenge the lack of authenticity in 'spirituality'? Jesus' biggest opposition throughout His ministry was always the religious. It remains the same for us today. Religion appears to be the way to God but tries to contain the One who is the Way. Religion prizes ritual over relationship, law over love.

When Jesus entered the temple, He set things straight. It's the same when He enters our lives, He drives out what has been robbing us of a right relationship with God, He turns over the deceit and lies we once believed, disrupts our tradition and challenges corruption and exploitation, highlighting the worthless sacrifice, as it says in Hosea 6:6, 'For I desire mercy, not sacrifice, and the acknowledgement of God rather than burnt offerings.' ('Acknowledgement' referring to loyalty or devotion, a genuine act of obedience in response to who God is).

Just like the children in the temple responded with praise, so does our inner child respond with praise to the revelation of King Jesus in the temple. Through the transforming work God does in us, we cannot help but feel thankful praise rise in us like a fountain that cannot be stopped.

When Jesus passionately enters the temple and puts things straight, He is restoring it to its intended purpose. He achieves the same in us. When we are restored through salvation, Jesus takes up residence in us and we become what we were designed to be, a temple of the Holy Spirit. Corruption is replaced with praise and selfishness is replaced with miracles. May we never be so caught up with religion that we forget what we are made to be and miss the wonderful, life transforming disruption that Jesus is doing in us (individually) and amongst us (corporately).

Prayer
Lord, I give You full access in my life. Disrupt and restore me. I pray that I will never compromise the purpose for which You made me. May praise be heard from this temple and healing flow to those who need it.

DAY 9: JUDGING YOURSELF UNWORTHY

Then Paul and Barnabas answered them boldly: We had to speak the word of God to you first. Since you rejected it and do not consider yourselves worthy of eternal life, we now turn to the Gentiles. Acts 13:46

Context
In Turkey, there were seventeen ancient cities named Antioch, on this occasion Paul and Barnabas were in Pisidian Antioch (v14), where they went into the synagogue on the Sabbath. Paul addressed the people present, taking them through their own history, revealing the good news of the promised Christ. Verse 45 says, 'When the Jews saw the crowds, they were filled with jealousy and talked abusively against what Paul was saying.' It is at this point that Paul and Barnabas made a statement that would have sent a shock wave through the entire crowd.

Today's Message
Let's read again what Paul and Barnabas said, but from the NKJV. "but since you rejected it and judge yourselves unworthy of everlasting life." Wow! Conversely, God calls us worthy of eternal life. Not through our own merit, but God made a way, 'while we were still sinners, Christ died for us' (Romans 5:8). In His mercy God calls us justified by His blood.

To reject this amazing good news of God's eternal rescue plan for humanity, is to be the judge of our own eternal destination. In our free will, we hold the power to accept or reject His salvation. God doesn't make the difficult decision as to whether we qualify for heaven or not, we do. Notice what Paul and Barnabas said almost sounds like reverse psychology. Allow me to paraphrase their words: 'You consider yourselves to be so important and well informed, proudly positioning yourselves above all other views, as though you have the monopoly on God. However, since your pride causes you to reject the good news of Jesus Christ, promised through your own scriptures, your best efforts at religion count for nothing. Therefore, you judge yourselves unworthy of eternal life and even position yourselves beneath us, the ones you despise. Instead the world will hear of God's salvation!' In Matthew 22:1-10 Jesus likens the kingdom of heaven to a man who arranges a wedding for his son, only for the guests to reject the invite, so he sent his servants to invite all they could find. No one is beyond the invitation to salvation.

The next time you share the gospel with someone, and they reject the message, remember that they are judging themselves unworthy of eternal life. Sad, but true. Your only responsibility is to simply share the good news, not twist anyone's arm. From there it's between them and the Holy Spirit, who is the only one who can complete the work of genuine salvation in someone's life. God does not want anyone to perish, but everyone to come to repentance (2 Peter 3:9). Whether they are successful and proud or homeless and broken, we are to take the message that they are precious and worthy of eternal life. What they do with it is up to them.

Prayer
Lord, although pride can get the better of me and it's easy to envy other people's success, You still see me as worthy of everlasting life. Thank You for Your salvation. Lead me to those whom You have prepared to hear and receive the gospel.

DAY 10: WHO DO YOU SAY I AM?

"But what about you?" He asked. "Who do you say I am?" Simon Peter answered, "You are the Christ, the Son of the living God." Matthew 16:15-16

Context

Verse 13-15 says, 'When Jesus came to the region of Caesarea Philippi, He asked His disciples, "Who do people say the Son of Man is?" They replied, "Some say John the Baptist; others say Elijah; still others, Jeremiah or one of the prophets." But what about you" He asked. "Who do you say I am?"' Jesus put the question to all His disciples, but only Simon answered. Perhaps because at that point, he was the only one who had received a revelation of Jesus's true identity.

Today's Message

It is extremely easy to go along with popular opinion, to blend in with the crowd, after all it says in verse 14, 'they replied'. It was the disciples who said, "Some say John the Baptist; others say Elijah; and still others, Jeremiah or one of the prophets." But when Jesus put the question to them all, "But what about you? Who do you say that I am?" It was Simon who replied, "You are the Christ, the Son of the living God." He could have simply kept his head down and followed the speculations of others. But this is a moment in Scripture where we see a revelation from the Father, through a work of the Holy Spirit that revealed the identity of Jesus, resulting in a confession. Romans 10:9 says, 'That if you confess with your mouth, "Jesus is Lord," and believe in your heart that God raised Him from the dead, you will be saved.' Confession and salvation go hand in hand. This is what we encounter through the Holy Spirit's work at the point of salvation when we receive a revelation of Jesus' identity causing us to make a 'confession of faith.' Followed by a lifestyle of worship in response to deeper revelations of who He is. Revelation from God will never supersede or contradict Scripture, but it will unveil a deeper understanding. What Peter received was a spirit awakening to the identity of Jesus already contained in Scripture.

Worship is not an opportunity to tell God who we are. All too often we make worship into 'a sensory experience' that is about us and what God has and will do for us. But true worship recognises that our salvation cost Him everything and it is His victory we live in every day. In verse 18, Jesus said, "And I tell you that you are Peter, and on this rock, I will build my church..." When we receive a revelation of who Jesus is, we also find our identity in Him. He gives us a renewed purpose in life and unlocks a future we never knew we had. Verse 17 says, 'Jesus replied, "Blessed are you, Simon son of Jonah, for this was not revealed to you by man, but by my Father in heaven."' Like Simon, your confession cannot be merely based on the opinions of others. What if those people were no longer around or they changed their opinion, would you change yours? If you think you would, I urge you to spend some time asking Jesus to reveal Himself to your heart.

Prayer

Lord, thank You for the revelation of who Jesus is through Your Holy Spirit. I confess You as my Lord and saviour. You are the Christ, the Son of the living God. I have my victory in You, not through my own doing, but by Your grace and mercy, so I can live with a new heavenly identity.

DAY 11: FORERUNNER OF FAITH

Because she thought, "If I just touch His clothes, I will be healed." Mark 5:28. They begged Him to let them touch even the edge of His cloak, and all who touched Him were healed. Mark 6:56b

Context
Before something is achieved, invented or built, it can seem impossible; something confined to the imagination. But have you ever noticed that once one person breaks through the limitations of possibility, it makes way for others to follow? This is exactly what happens in Mark 5 and 6.

Today's Message
As we read the gospels, we see healing activated by faith. This passage (Mark 5:24-34) was one such occasion. An unnamed woman gets Jesus' attention and her healing because she acted on her belief that Jesus was the Messiah spoken of in Malachi 4:2: 'But to you who fear My name, the Sun of Righteousness shall arise with healing in His wings' (NKJV). The wings (outer corners) were where the tassels with blue thread hung, instructed by God to Moses to wear for all generations (Numbers 15:37-41). There was healing in Jesus' wings, but reaching out to touch Him had not been done before, she was the forerunner. Her action took the word of God at its word, which gave her the faith to reach out and receive her healing. Romans 10:17 says, 'so then faith comes by hearing, and hearing by the word of God' (NKJV). She not only received her healing but her dignity too. No longer socially excluded, she could rebuild her life.

The woman had tried every doctor available, with no success. The first chance she had to reach out to Jesus, she took it. You too might have tried every option before turning to Jesus. By which point feelings of guilt for not turning to Him sooner become a blockage of your own making. The Lord wants you to know that it is not too late, you should not let guilt or the limitations of your understanding of God's grace hold you back from reaching out for your healing from Jesus.

You have probably read this passage many times before, but what makes it even more fascinating is the last verse of chapter 6 which says, 'They begged Him to let them touch even the edge of His cloak, and all who touched Him were healed. Faith now was not just waiting for Jesus to touch them; they could reach out to touch Him. As a result, verse 56 says, 'all who touched Him were healed.' Here Romans 10:17 suddenly comes to life, miracles came out of faith; faith came from hearing the testimony of the woman's simple act of faith based on the word of God.

The effect of your testimony is powerful and far reaching. You may never know the extent of the impact your life can have on others, even if no one knows your name. This does not mean you cannot be used by God, to raise someone's faith to receive their miracle. Act on the word of God, seize your moment and be the forerunner that sees God do amazing things in others.

Prayer
Lord, your word says I can reach out to You by faith for my miracle. Let my faith be a witness that stirs the faith in others to unlock their understanding of what Your word says we are entitled to, as heirs of Your kingdom. Keys that will bring transformation and healing to many.

DAY 12: SOMETHING HAPPENED

When Jesus reached the spot, he looked up and said to him, "Zacchaeus, come down immediately. I must stay at your house today. Luke 19:5
Jesus said to him, "Today salvation has come to this house, because this man, too, is a son of Abraham. Luke 19:9 (of 19:1-10)

Context
In Mark 10:46, it says 'Then they came to Jericho. As Jesus and His disciples, together with a large crowd were leaving the city...' I have heard it preached that Jesus entered the city of Jericho and nothing caught His attention, so they left again and that's when Jesus came across Bartimaeus. But Luke 19:1-10 is talking about the same occasion in Jericho (leading up to Jesus going to Jerusalem). Mark's supposed omission of Zacchaeus could be explained by the fact that the ancient city of Jericho was for the most part abandoned and a new Jericho, built by Herod the Great, was just south of the old one. This would explain the confusion over whether Jesus was entering Jericho (Luke) or leaving (Matthew and Mark) when He met Zacchaeus, depending on which city the writers were referring to.

Today's Message
Zacchaeus' wealth did not hold any sway over getting the crowd to give him a prominent front row view in preparation for Jesus passing by. He would have been well known, but for all the wrong reasons. That's how much tax collectors were despised, and he was a chief of tax collectors!
If you were that despised and an A-lister celebrity picked you out of a crowd to hang out with him, would you say no? Zacchaeus may have felt smug, even boastful that he had been chosen over everyone else, but Jesus wasn't looking to boost Zacchaeus' social status; He had another agenda. Zacchaeus was branded a 'sinner', but he was about to have a salvation encounter with the 'friend of sinners.'

Anyone seeing Jesus at Zacchaeus' house would have assumed that Jesus was the guest, but it was Jesus who did the inviting. When Jesus calls us, it's us who must make room for Him in our lives. Salvation brings change – life transforming change. Zacchaeus' response to Jesus showed that his security was no longer in his wealth. He was even prepared to back date his wrongs. Verse 9 says, 'Jesus said to him, "Today salvation has come to this house"' In a western culture, the gospel is sadly often sold as an individual's self-help solution with eternal benefits, but his transformation impacted the whole household and the community. True salvation isn't personal, it's to be shared. It brings inward change that lived out brings transformation in the community. You just can't hold it inside. The rest of verse 9 says, "because this man, too, is a son of Abraham." Jesus not only had brought salvation but had declared to all those watching that Zacchaeus was one of them, giving back his dignity, helping others to see past the job and recognise that this man too was a brother.

Prayer
Jesus, I pray that You will help me to open my life and my home to true salvation that will cause shockwaves, reaching to the parameters of my world of influence and beyond. I refuse to contain my salvation, but allow it to impact my family, friends, community and world in Jesus' name.

DAY 13: MAKE A NOISE

When he heard that it was Jesus of Nazareth, be began to shout. "Jesus, Son of David, have mercy on me!" Many rebuked him and told him to be quiet, but he shouted all the more, "Son of David, have mercy on me!" Jesus stopped and said, "call him." Mark 10:47-49 (46-52)

Context
Beggars at the side of the road were not uncommon and Jesus would have passed many as He went from town to town, city to city. This occasion would have been no different, except for the fact that one beggar, Bartimaeus, hearing Jesus of Nazareth was passing by, knew through a revelation He was in fact the Son of David (a Messianic title). The blind man seeing his opportunity called out for the healer's attention. Bartimaeus recognised what many failed to see.

Today's Message
Do you have a need, a limitation that is holding you back, pushing you to the wayside? The Cambridge Dictionary defines 'wayside' as, 'If someone falls by the wayside, they fail to finish an activity'. Do you feel like there is more still inside you, more to give, but you are held down by circumstances and told to shut up and put up? Bartimaeus' status could have defined him, held him in his place. But his desperation for change, coupled with a revelation that Jesus is the promised Messiah from the Scriptures (possibly read before losing his sight or heard read in the synagogue), ignited faith, that caused him to make a noise that made Jesus stop.

The same people who tried to shut Bartimaeus up moments earlier, were now telling him to cheer up. Jesus was surrounded by those who thought they had the monopoly on Him. But Jesus responds to faith – loud, undignified, pride abandoned, mould breaking, noise making, action taking faith! Jesus did not call Bartimaeus over, He told the very ones who were shutting him up to call him over. Jesus was showing them that He responds to faith, not piety. He demolished their idea of in-crowds and cliques; class divides and status. Are you prepared to make some noise? Not only will Jesus respond to your faith, but He will challenge those around you in the process.

Bartimaeus makes another statement of faith by throwing his cloak aside. How would he find it again if he did not receive his sight? He had no guarantee, did he? Bartimaeus wanted change and was prepared to walk away from everything that was familiar. But we are mistaken if we think faith is found in wanting something badly enough that we blindly *step out* from our circumstances. Rather, Faith is found in the *stepping in* to a total trust in Jesus. In verse 51 Jesus asks, "What do you want me to do for you?" Obvious right? It was not that Jesus didn't know what he needed, but He was drawing Bartimaeus into completing this transaction of faith for healing by effectively saying, "Okay, you have my attention, don't waste this opportunity, be specific because there is power in verbalising your need to Me." Bartimaeus had to speak out his request for all to hear. Keeping your need private for fear or doubt is not faith. Faith is an outward declaration to God and those around you about where you put your trust. You have His attention, don't waste it.

Prayer
Lord, You know my circumstance (add your own), I'm making a noise to You, because You are the one I believe can change and transform anything. I throw off the old and come to You.

DAY 14: BY WHAT AUTHORITY?

"By what authority are you doing these things? They asked. "And who gave you authority to do this?" Mark 11:28 (27-33)

Context
Earlier in chapter eleven, Jesus had cleared the temple the day before, driving out those buying and selling by turning over tables and benches, and preventing anyone from carrying merchandise through the temple. Wow! If you had an image of Jesus meek and mild, scrap it. Jesus is passionate about what matters. The chief priests and the teachers of the law didn't question whether Jesus was right to do what He did; they wanted to know; 1. By what authority? and 2. Who gave Him the authority? Jesus hadn't been schooled by a Rabbi and therefore lacked human authority.

Today's Message
'By what authority' is a question we often ask of others: Who gave you the right? Aren't you a bit young to be teaching me? What are his credentials? Where did she train? Is it possible that we too can slip into the mentality of the chief priests and the teachers of the law?

As we read this passage, we support Jesus' actions, but what if someone 'turned over the tables in our world'. In other words, what if they challenged our traditions and questioned the customs in church we hold to so dearly? We know what they are saying isn't wrong, but we don't like how they said it or the fact that they are not ordained. After all, who do they think they are? By what authority dare they challenge me? And who gave them that authority?

How would we react if someone turned over the book stall at the back of church or the monthly Fair-Trade stall? What if they disrupted the lucrative café in church or the worship album studio? Would they be wrong? We might use these things to resource the church, but what if the Holy Spirit said "stop" and used someone 'unauthorised' to say it? Would we pay attention? Whether these things are right or wrong is not in question here, but our ability to discern what is from God. These things should not be judged based on opinions, books or even consulting YouTube! Knowing right and wrong is discerned through the Holy Spirit. 1 Corinthians 2:14 says 'The man without the Spirit does not accept the things that come from the Spirit of God, for they are foolishness to him, and cannot understand them, because they are spiritually discerned'. As Christians we have the Holy Spirit and therefore we can listen to what He has to say on the matter. Before you make your next complaint, spend time in prayer, ask the Lord to show you whether it is of God or not? Should it be challenged? As Acts 5:39 says, 'But if it is from God, you will not be able to stop these men; you will only find yourself fighting against God.'

Prayer
Lord, I pray for discernment from the Holy Spirit. Help me to not judge others but recognise who has Your authority. Show me the traditions I hold so precious and help me to let them go. Give me the wisdom to know when I am wrong and the grace to admit it.

DAY 15: BROKEN TO RELEASE

While He was in Bethany, reclining at the table in the home of a man known as Simon the Leper, a woman came with an alabaster jar of very expensive perfume, made of pure nard. She broke the jar and poured the perfume on His head. **Mark 14:3 (3-11)**

Context
There is a lot in this passage that has been drawn out many times before. But notice that she broke the jar. Not only was her act of worship extremely expensive, but more to the point, it was symbolic of an irreversible sacrifice - her sacrifice to Jesus. Like the jar, her value was not on the outside and Jesus, in an earlier moment, helped her to see her inner value as a child of God. The woman's irreversible sacrifice was in response to her irreversible life transformation.

Today's Message
If the woman had simply opened the jar and poured the content on Jesus, she would have still given away something of great value, but her sacrifice wasn't about giving a costly offering, it was about the irreversible abandonment of a previous life symbolic through a simple broken jar.

So long as the jar remained intact, it could revert to its previous use. If she too held anything back, she was effectively keeping the door open to the potential of returning to a previous life of sin. When the jar was broken, all the perfume would have poured out, nothing could be held back. The broken jar showed Jesus, she was holding nothing back. As a result, the value, beauty and potential from within had been fully released. In the same way, all of herself was poured out.

It is at the point of pouring out that the greatest impact for the kingdom of God is achieved. After all, even God poured out. Jesus said in Matthew 26:28 "This is my blood of the covenant, which is poured out for many for the forgiveness of sins." When Jesus was poured out as a sacrifice, it was the single most powerful demonstration of love the world had and would ever see. If God hadn't already given enough, He was still prepared to pour out His Spirit, recorded by Luke in Acts 10:45. It's only then that the church's true potential in Him is released. When we pour out of ourselves as a sacrifice, completely reliant and emptied to God, we are at our most effective.

Jesus said in verse 9 "I tell you the truth, wherever the gospel is preached throughout the world, what she has done will also be told, in memory of her." What a legacy! Sacrifice creates its own legacy. There is power in the sacrifice that we cannot equate. If we could measure its impact, many people would wrongly trade with it to advance their 'ministry', thereby misunderstanding the whole point of sacrifice. God wants our all; nothing held back; no plan B if God doesn't give you what you want. He is looking for a people that are prepared to leave the old life behind and 'offer your bodies as living sacrifices, holy and pleasing to God.' (Romans 12:1). to be irreversibly broken in response to Jesus, who is our ultimate sacrifice.

Prayer
Lord Jesus, I pray that I may never equate sacrifice with gain but pour myself out as an irreversible offering to You, in response to a life transformed. There is no sin that I have committed that puts me beyond Your reach. My response to Your salvation is an abandoned pouring out of myself.

DAY 16: THE SPIRIT REVEALS MY FOUNDATION

Therefore, everyone who hears these words of mine and puts them into practice is like a wise man who built his house on the rock. The rain came down, the streams rose, and the winds blew and beat against that house; yet it did not fall, because it had its foundation on the rock. **Matthew 7:24-25**

Context
Whilst reading this passage, I was struck by three words in verses 24 and 27, rain, streams and winds. Somehow we translate these words to mean a storm with the intent to cause destruction. This is because we see storms depicted elsewhere in Scripture as bad things and therefore assume this passage depicts a trial by storm that comes from the world or the enemy. But in this passage, Jesus doesn't mention a storm, trial or the enemy.

Today's Message
What if, in this passage, Jesus was talking about the Holy Spirit testing our foundations? After all, the Spirit of God throughout Scripture is described as coming like rain, a stream and wind.

Rain: "I will pour out My Spirit on your offspring, and my blessing on your descendants. They will spring up like grass in a meadow, like poplar trees by flowing streams." Isaiah 44:3b-4.

Stream: '"Whoever believes in Me, as the Scripture has said, streams of living water will flow from within him." By this he meant the Spirit...' John 7:38
'The man brought me back to the entrance to the temple, and I saw water coming out from under the threshold of the temple.' Ezekiel 47:1.

Wind: 'Suddenly a sound like the blowing of a violent wind came from heaven and filled the whole house where they were sitting' Acts 2:2.
'For He will come like a pent-up flood that the breath of the Lord drives along.' Isaiah 59:19.

What if Jesus was talking about when the Spirit is poured out; flows from the temple; and shakes things up, causing our foundation to be exposed and reveals where we put our trust. We have no problem accepting Hebrews 12:5-6 that talks about God disciplining those He loves, or John 15:1-8 that describes us as branches He prunes to produce more fruit. So, could this passage actually be depicting the Spirit at work to radically challenge where we place our trust and expose our foundations? This is an act of love by God to ensure our trust isn't misplaced but grounded on the Word, Christ Jesus our rock, so when persecution or trials come, we are able to stand strong.

Will we be found standing strong, having established our faith on the Word of God? It is not a matter of reciting Scripture, but as Jesus said in verse 24, it's about putting His words into practice. He is serious about our commitment and challenges us to build our lives on the solid foundation of Himself, our Chief Cornerstone (Ephesians 2:20). So, when His Spirit is poured out, flows like a river or blows like a wind, we do not crumble and fall away, but hear and obey the Word of God and respond in partnership to the mission of the Holy Spirit.

Prayer
Lord, I welcome Your Holy Spirit. Help me to recognise when it is You challenging me to build my life on You alone and nothing else. Help me to remove any unstable foundations so I will stand firm on Your word alone.

DAY 17: I AM WILLING

A man with leprosy came to Him and begged Him on his knees, "If you are willing, you can make me clean." Filled with compassion, Jesus reached out His hand and touched the man. "I am willing," He said, "Be clean!" Immediately the leprosy left him, and he was cured. Mark 1:40-42

Context
By touching the man with leprosy, Jesus would by Mosaic law, become unclean Himself. However, Jesus reached out His hand and touched the man. There was no question in his mind about whether Jesus could heal him. The question was about willingness. Would Jesus be willing to help a diseased social outcast who was to be avoided at all cost.

Jesus was filled with compassion. He did not just feel a bit of compassion or thought it would look good in front of His followers. He was 'filled' with a compassion that effectively consumed Him in that moment. True compassion is a spiritual impartation by God, that exceeds human efforts and compels us to reach out and touch the untouchable; love the unlovable; and enter someone's world in the confidence of the power of God. I would suggest that in this passage we see Jesus responding to the Father's heart, through an impartation of compassion by the Holy Spirit.

Today's Message
There were occasions when Jesus approached individuals, for example, when He healed the lame man (John 5:1-15) and raise the widow's son to life (Luke 7:11-17). But, more often than not, Jesus seems to set a principle that the key to faith is coming to Him, not waiting for Him to come to them. Faith compelled the man to leave his comfort zone, walk amongst the 'clean' and even fall to his knees in front of the crowd and beg. Lack of faith says, "Jesus knows what I need, if He loves me, he will come to me." No one has the monopoly on Jesus or knows a formula for a miracle, but we do see in Scripture time and time again that Jesus responds to faith that seeks Him out and gets His attention.

Begging is undignified, it causes a scene, it makes you look needy, even dependant on someone else for something in their power to give. This is what the man with leprosy was prepared to do. Something we admire him for but are often too proud to do ourselves. We do not want to bother Jesus with our 'insignificant request', and call it being humble. I dread to think how much we struggle with because we don't want to bother God with it. Are you waiting for Jesus to come to you? Maybe today is the day you go to Jesus. Yes, He knows what you need before you ask, but this is not about God knowing what we need, it's about us asking, because faith gives us the courage to approach His throne and ask boldly (Philippians 4:6-7). Even if it is motivated by desperation and it feels like a selfish request, Scripture shows us that bold prayers and action gets the Lord's attention (1 Chronicles 4:9-10, Luke 5:20, Luke 11:5-13). What have you got to lose?

Prayer
Lord, I put aside my pride. Forgive me for hiding in the comfort zone of unbelief. Lord, teach me how to come to You, prepared to do what it takes to see a miracle. Thank You that You are willing.

DAY 18: ACCOUNTABLE

When I say to a wicked man, 'you will surely die,' and you do not warn him or speak out to dissuade him from his evil ways in order to save his life, that wicked man will die for his sin, and I will hold you accountable for his blood. Ezekiel 3:18 (16-21)

Context

Chapter three of Ezekiel is so relevant and powerful for us today that it leaps off the page and grabs the evangelist's heart. Ezekiel was charged with the responsibility of warning God's people of their sin. It is well worth reading the six verses of this passage, but allow me to break it down:

Evil person commits sin. You do not warn them = no opportunity to turn from sin = death for their sin and you are accountable (verse 18).

Evil person commits sin. You do warn them = opportunity to turn from sin, but they reject it = death for their sin, but you save yourself (verse 19).

The same is true of a righteous person who falls into sin...

Righteous person falls into sin. You do not warn them = death for their sin and you are accountable (verse 20).

Righteous person falls into sin. You do warn them, and they turn from sin = life and you will have saved yourself (verse 21).

Today's Message

This passage is so clear and leaves no doubt that the great commission is for us to be like a watchman (verse 16). A watchman's role is to stand on the wall and look for anyone approaching. If they failed in their duty to warn the people to prepare if they came under attack, they were accountable and could often be put to death. That is what is happening here in this passage, God calls Ezekiel to be the one to warn the people to turn from sin.

If we allow ourselves to be consumed by our own lives: image, career, ministry etc, we will be held accountable for those we do not warn. This passage 'doesn't beat around the bush.' We are required to warn people that they are under attack from sin which leads to spiritual death. Galatians 6:1 says 'Brothers, if someone is caught in a sin, you who are spiritual should restore him gently. But watch yourself, or you also may be tempted.' The religious are not called to restore a brother, otherwise they might require penance to restore them through works. But the spiritual who are connected to the Father's compassionate heart are required to restore their brother in love.

Prayer

Lord, may I not be content with my own salvation alone, but warn those in my circle of influence to turn from sin and come to You. Grant me the opportunities to speak and the words to say, in love and grace, with an urgency in my heart that knows it is a matter of spiritual life or death.

DAY 19: THE FATHER'S HEART

This is how God showed His love among us: He sent His one and only Son into the world that we might live through Him. This is love: not that we loved God, but that He loved us and sent His Son as an atoning sacrifice for our sins. Dear friends, since God so loved us, we also ought to love one another. **1 John 4:9-11**

Context

I was eighteen and had just returned from a Baptist Union youth weekend in South Wales, to a house in Barrow-Upon-Soar in Leicestershire, where myself and a friend were housesitting for a young couple who had travelled to Brazil for the summer to help build an orphanage. I put my bags down in my bedroom and sat down, tired from the journey. As I sat in the chair, I found myself watching an amazing sunset through the window across the room from me. At that moment the Lord spoke and said, "You are going to heaven." He then drew my attention to the window to my right. Across the garden were some tennis courts where some teenagers were playing tennis. The Lord then said, "But they are not." I instantly broke down in tears and cried uncontrollably for about an hour.

Today's Message

I did not know those boys. And if I am honest, on a personal level, I didn't particularly care. But God showed me His heart for those who do not know Him. His heart breaks for every one of them. He longs to be in relationship with those He made in His image. When God shows you His heart for the lost, you know that church could never just be for the religious.

I have told this story several times and every time I do, I cry as I sense the Holy Spirit reminding me of the Father's heart. Ever since I said 'yes' to the calling into youth work, in whatever form that has taken; secular or Christian, I know that God has opened doors and given me an anointing to do the work. This does not mean that I am the best youth worker and it certainly doesn't mean I get it right all of the time. But feeling God's breaking heart for young people who do not know Him, motivates me and enables me to know that He will use my words and actions beyond what I am naturally capable of.

You may have never experienced a sense of calling, which has left you frustrated and feeling abandoned by God. But is it possible that you have simply overlooked what the Holy Spirit has been stirring within you? God has not forgotten you. Take some time out to ask Him to reawaken a sense of the Father's heart. Calling is not just about doing stuff for God; it's about living in response to His heart. When you know your calling, you enter a partnership with God that requires you to give it your best and He supernaturally adds a dimension that brings a bigger impact than we could ever manufacture ourselves. Ask Him to show you what breaks His heart.

Prayer

Father God, break my heart for what breaks Yours. Out of which, I pray I will live my life in response to this awakened calling that sees an anointing to make an impact in the lives of others, far beyond what I could ever achieve myself.

DAY 20: PETITION

Do not be anxious about anything, but in everything, by prayer and petition, with thanksgiving, present your requests to God. And the peace of God, which transcends all understanding, will guard your hearts and your minds in Christ Jesus. Philippians 4:6-7

Context
The Greek word deēsei appears five times in the New Testament and is where we get the word supplication, implying a humble and earnest request to God. In the NIV version of the Bible, the word has been translated as petition.

Today's Message
When I think of a petition, I think of someone asking me to agree with what they are proposing to take to the Government or a large corporation as a form of request for change or an objection against injustice. To show my support, I would add my name to their petition, which formally backs their request, giving them a greater chance of being heard and bringing about a change.

All too often, we pray and ask God for something, but it is a private request, and if God was to turn us down, we haven't lost face. After all we don't like our pride to be dented. But to present our prayers and petitions to God paints a picture in my mind of going to my brothers and sisters in Christ and asking them to agree with me. This requires a certain level of risk because it exposes what I need God to do. But by sharing my petition with others, it does five things:

1. It brings my request to Godly wisdom, allowing other believers to correct, even rebuke me if my prayers are selfish or unscriptural.
2. It increases my confidence to come to God in prayer and ask something of Him, when I have the backing of men and women of God who are behind me.
3. By highlighting the need, more believers will bring the same prayers to God.
4. It demonstrates a higher level of faith and expectancy. 'And my God will meet all your needs according to His glorious riches in Christ Jesus (Philippians 4:19).
5. It demonstrates the power of agreement. Matthew 18:19 says, "Again, I tell you that if two of you on earth agree about anything you ask for, it will be done for you by My Father in heaven. For where two or three come together in My name, there am I with them."

Wow! When we are in agreement with other faith-filled believers, we know our petition has stood the test and we can confidently bring our petition to God. Let us then approach the throne of grace with confidence, so that we may receive mercy and find grace to help us in our time of need (Hebrews 4:16).

Prayer
Lord, I am excited about bringing my prayers and petitions to You, my Living God, who hears my prayers. May I have the confidence to be vulnerable before other believers, the grace to accept their wisdom, and the boldness to approach Your throne in unity.

DAY 21: DELIGHT YOURSELF

Delight yourself in the Lord and He will give you the desires of your heart. (Psalm 37:4)

Context
I have heard this verse quoted out of context so many times, as though it's a ticket for asking God for anything we desire. Who wouldn't want to sign up to a God like that?! But what happens is that we only focus on: 'He will give you the desires of your heart.' It is true, but only if we couple it with the preceding words of the same verse, 'Delight yourself in the Lord and…' This verse contains a lock and key. The Key is the delight, the lock is the desires. We must take the key to release the lock. But it's not a 'do this and you'll get what you want' scenario…

Today's Message
Not all desires in our hearts are God given. Therefore, not all desires are good for us. It can often be difficult to distinguish between godly and personal desires, so it's important to 1. share your heart's desires with godly people you trust, who can pray and decern with you, and 2. Listen to what comes out of your mouth. Luke 6:45 says, 'For out of the overflow of his heart his mouth speaks.' Our words reveal what is in our heart. In other words, the things we say 'off the record' exposes who we really are, what motivates us and what we really think and believe. Our words can either speak life to transform or jeopardise our desires.

I think there is a principle at play here that says you can create your own world, based on your words. If you believe it, you'll speak it and are then more likely to act on it. So, it becomes a self-fulfilling prophesy. Whether it's positive or negative, words of life or death, blessing or curse, there are one of two outcomes, those who delight themselves in the Lord and those who do not. Both receiving what is in their heart. Godly desires leading to satisfaction, purpose and fullness of life. Or selfish desires that lead to deep dissatisfaction, consumerism and destruction.

God delights our hearts when we let Him in. 'Be transformed by the renewing of your mind. Then you will be able to test and approve what God's will is – His good, pleasing and perfect will.' (Romans 12:2). He fills our hearts with what He desires. Other desires fade away. His will becomes our will, His desires and priorities become ours too. It is then that we move away from selfish desires and move towards God's will. What we pursue changes and so do our prayers, as we begin to move into a place of agreement with Almighty God, and He responds with a yes and amen. Jesus said in Luke 11:13, '…how much more will Your Father in heaven give the Holy Spirit to those who ask Him.' As parents, we want to give good gifts *to* our children, but God gives a gift that is good *for* His children. Jesus is not saying our efforts are rubbish and God is trying to outdo us, He is saying that the best gift you could receive is the gift of the Holy Spirit. When we delight ourselves in Him, we agree that there is nothing more satisfying than the Holy Spirit and out of Him comes all we could desire. And the beauty of it is that there is no limit!

Prayer
Lord, help me to put my delight in You and nowhere else. Search my heart and reveal what needs to go. I set my priorities on You and desire Your Holy Spirit in accordance with your will.

DAY 22: POWER TO THE PEOPLE

And will not God bring about justice for His chosen ones, who cry out to Him day and night? Will He keep putting them off? I tell you, He will see that they get justice, and quickly. However, when the Son of Man comes, will He find faith on the earth?
Luke 18:7-8 (1-8)

Context
In Luke, chapters 16-18, Jesus lifts the beggar, the leper, the widow and the child. At that time, these were the lowest of the low in society. They had no influence on how they were viewed or power to change how they were treated. The construct of society had assigned them their place. But Jesus gives a place in heaven for the beggar, healing to the leper, a voice to the widow and welcomes the little children to Him and declares that this is exactly how we should come to Him.

It seems strange that Jesus would liken an unjust judge to God. But He is illustrating that if even an unjust judge would respond to persistency of the voiceless and powerless; how much more will God respond to us, His chosen ones. Jesus invites His disciples to get serious; to take their praying to another level by never giving up. Will Jesus find that sort of persistency in us?

Today's Message
Once again we find a key and a lock. The key is the crying out day and night. And the lock to be opened is the receiving of justice. This therefore is a promise that God will respond with justice to those who persist. The problem we have, is that very often, we just can't be bothered to put that much effort in; we forget; we give up too soon; or we simply don't think that we should have to ask so many times. This leaves us in a deficit of faith and expectation that comes short of seeing the possibilities which can be achieved through persistent prayer.

Jesus is not talking about the persistent prince, general or priest. But He uses the illustration of a voiceless and powerless widow. Yes, Jesus is talking about being persistent in prayer to God. But maybe it's more than that? Maybe Jesus is also saying that anyone can be a world changer. History shows us that the world changers were the ones who saw injustice and challenged it. They hit obstacles time and time again; as well as personal criticism and often violence, until eventually breakthrough came. If something is worth fighting for, then it's worth persevering for.

Jesus is giving power to the people. After all, the well quoted verse of Micah 6:8 says that, 'To act justly, and to love mercy and to walk humbly with your God' should be enough to stir a fire in us to stand in the gap and respond with justice. Conversely, to stay silent is to let injustice continue, with the hope that someone else will deal with it. But what if God is nudging you to step up and be like the persistent widow. It takes motivation and determination to change a situation, it starts with one prayer or one phone call, then the next and the next until breakthrough comes.

Prayer
Lord Jesus, thank You for revealing the keys to Your kingdom. Each key allowing me to unlock more of an understanding of who You are and who I am in You. Lord, help me to stand against injustice. Thank You that I have power in my voice, and You encourage me to use it.

DAY 23: THANK YOU!

One of them, when he saw he was healed, came back, praising God in a loud voice. He threw himself at Jesus' feet and thanked Him. Luke 17:15

Context
It's very easy to get what we want and never give a thought to where it came from or be thankful. We often take things for granted, especially when we think we have worked hard enough to get it ourselves. But if God was to show us just how much He is involved in our lives, I think we would be embarrassed to admit how ungrateful we really are. Leprosy 2,000 years ago was incurable, so to be healed would have meant so much. Not only would they have got back their physical appearance, but could also re-enter society, return to their families, resume their trade and enter the temple. But having much to be thankful for doesn't guarantee thankfulness.

Today's Message
In verse 18, Jesus asks, "Was no-one found to return and give praise to God except this foreigner?" He wasn't despising the Samaritan, but expressing His disappointment in the others, assumedly Jewish men who were merely following Jesus' instruction to go and show themselves to the priests; a law the Lord Himself gave to Moses in Leviticus 14. At which point, the priest would examine the man and declare him cleansed before he could return to normal life. Instead, this man came and fell at Jesus' feet and Jesus, in verse 19 said, "Rise and go; your faith has made you well." By saying this, Jesus was declaring Himself to be the Great High Priest (Hebrews 4:14), authorised by God to examine and declare the man cleansed.

The Samaritan man gives us a great example of how not to get carried along with the crowd or stuck in a ceremonial ritual, thereby not missing the One we are in the presence of. He wasn't prepared to take his healing and go without first praising God and giving thanks to whom thanks was due. We could speculate that the other nine went off and fulfilled the law's requirements and then in some way privately thanked God. But I've heard people say, "I like to worship God in my own way." Which usually translates as they are too uncomfortable to praise God publicly or don't actually have a relationship with Jesus at all. But in this passage, we see the man who once had to stand at a distance, now worshipping at Jesus' feet with an overflowing expression of a thankful heart. Thankfulness brings us close to Jesus in worship. The more thankful we are, the more we won't to express it. Perhaps you struggle to 'enter into' worship? Take some time to consider how thankful you are towards God. Acknowledge where your help comes from, who protects you and who provides for all your needs. The more we practice saying 'thank you' to God and admit our dependency on Him, the more our self-reliance fades away.

Prayer
Lord Jesus, open my eyes to see what you have done in my life and what you continue to do, so that my heart will overflow with thankfulness in worship at Your feet.

DAY 24: HAVE A GO IF YOU THINK YOU'RE GOOD ENOUGH

When Jesus heard this, He said to him, "You still lack one thing. Sell everything you have and give to the poor, and you will have treasure in heaven. Then come follow me." Luke 18:22(18-25)

Context
He was successful, rich and by his own account - kept the law. Surely that was enough to guarantee this ruler a place near the front of the line for inheriting eternal life. But he was asking Jesus from the perspective of works. If inheriting eternal life was based on his own efforts, Jesus would have most likely welcomed him into the flock there and then. Afterall, the rich ruler would have been a great financial sponsor and political ally to have on the team. But that wasn't a perspective Jesus would entertain, because His dependency was on the Father alone.

Today's Message
If you are striving to be good enough for God, save your energy. We could never earn our way into eternal life. And if you think that you need to hold on to your place in heaven by meeting certain criteria, then you have missed the point of the gospel of grace.

I imagine the rich ruler expected Jesus to respond with words of impressed congratulations and a public acknowledgement to all those stood nearby that he had earned his ticket into heaven. But if you are trying to earn your way, there will always be something else you could do. Have a go if you think you're good enough! But religion without Jesus offers nothing more than the carrot and stick, forever grasping for assurance of your salvation, just for it to be forever out of reach. The gospel, on the other hand, starts from a place of God being good (v18). Ephesians 2:8 says, 'For it is by grace you have been saved, through faith – and this not from yourselves, it is the gift of God – not by works, so that no-one can boast.'

We always feel that we have to do more or be more, and anything less is failure? Let's read verse 16-17 of Luke 18, 'But Jesus called the children to Him and said, "Let the little children come to Me, and do not hinder them, for the kingdom of God belongs to such as these. I tell you the truth, anyone who will not receive the kingdom of God like a little child will never enter it."' What a contrast to the rich ruler. We must stop complicating the gospel. Turning it into a set of criteria that we so readily place on ourselves and others in order to display some form of credibility or spiritual maturity. Verse 27 tells us that it's impossible to enter heaven on human effort, but possible with God. Jesus has done all that was necessary for us to inherit eternal life. Our King has paid the price that we may receive it for free. Salvation is God's specialty, not ours. All we have to do is receive it.

Prayer
Lord, help me to understand how to come to you as a little child and to not over complicate the gospel with things that don't matter, striving for acceptance from the One who already accepts me.

DAY 25: DEPENDENCY

Ask and it will be given to you; seek and you will find; knock and the door will be opened to you. For everyone who asks receives; he who seeks finds; and to him who knocks, the door will be opened. Matthew 7:7-9

Context
In this passage, Jesus goes on to talk about gifts that we give to our children if they ask. As such, there are a few things we often consider first as parents: will it spoil them? And do we have the resources to provide it? In Matthew 6:8 Jesus said, "your Father knows what you need before you ask Him." Therefore, He knows what's best for us and whether it fits with His will for our lives. And should you be in any doubt, He has all the resources required to provide for our needs. God does not need a payment plan. You could never leave Him bankrupt or out of ideas.

Today's Message
My biggest question is then, why does the Bible tell me that God says yes, when the answer seems to be no? Does it feel like God is saying no to you? How does that leave you feeling? Sadly, most of us blame God for unanswered prayers, rather than looking to identify what might be the real cause. Maybe we are asking for the wrong thing? Or asking for the right thing but expecting God to answer in a certain way or within a certain time frame. Maybe our idea of what we need isn't God's idea. Could it also be that we are living in disobedience to God?

Perhaps you are feeling stressed and as a result you can feel the stress starting to affect your body, which only increases the stress levels further as you see no way out of your situation. Let us remind ourselves of these powerful verses in Philippians 4:6-7. 'Do not be anxious about anything, but in everything, by prayer and petition, with thanksgiving, present your requests to God. And the peace of God, which transcends all understanding, will guard your hearts and your minds in Christ Jesus.

Faith is key to our prayers. But maybe faith shouldn't just be understood as 'trust' or 'hope' but read as 'dependency.' Dependency on God is a lifestyle. Maybe it isn't just what we say, but the dependency we come to Him with. When we are dependent like a little child, we recognise where our help comes from. We become expectant – isn't that what faith is? In that relationship, a child isn't afraid to ask, even persist, because their parent is the source of all their needs. Let that sink in for a moment and consider how your relationship with your heavenly Father is or could be.

Ask, seek, knock. Let God hear your prayers. Come with expectancy that is birthed out of dependency on Him. Stop exhausting yourself trying all other options or solving all your problems before turning to Jesus. Spend time in His presence and check your prayers against what you know to be God's will. Lay your life before Him, with all your hopes and dreams, needs and desires. Allow the Holy Spirit to minister to you, inspire your prayers and lift your burdens.

Prayer
Lord, I am totally dependent on You, more than I could ever realise. Help me to come to You like a little child and ask, seek, knock with expectancy and lay everything before you.

DAY 26: WHY DIDN'T I SEE THAT

As they talked and discussed these things with each other, Jesus Himself came up and walked along with them; but they were kept from recognising Him. Luke 24:15-16

Context

Jesus had appeared to the women by the tomb early on Sunday morning, and the twelve in the locked room. He was even recognised by Peter and the disciples out fishing on the lake when Jesus stood on the shore before cooking them breakfast. Yet, these two disciples, not of the twelve, Cleopas and an unnamed man, were not stupid and would have undoubtedly recognised Jesus for the considerable length of time they spent with Him on the seven mile walk from Jerusalem to Emmaus. However, they had been prevented from recognising Him (v16) until 'When He was at the table with them, He took bread, gave thanks, broke it and began to give it to them. Then their eyes were opened, and they recognised Him, and He disappeared from their sight.' (v30-31).

Today's Message

It can sometimes feel like everyone else gets to witness the miraculous, but we somehow miss it. We blame ourselves for not being 'spiritual' enough, as though we can earn it. You may not understand what is going on in your life right now, you may be confused, even disappointed with the way things have turned out. That's how these two disciples felt. As frustrating as it can be to feel on the outside of everything, let me encourage you, Jesus is nearer than you think, even if you don't recognise Him. We often look for Jesus in the big life-transforming moments, but He is closer than that. Most of the time, we don't feel anything. Then there are times when His presence is so evident, our bodies have a physiological or emotional reaction to His presence. Some people shake, I on the other hand cry. Like these disciples, some people's hearts burn or pound in their chest. Whatever it is for you, allow that to be your indicator that you are in the presence of the King. Verse 32 says, 'They asked each other, "Were not our hearts burning within us while He talked with us on the road and opened the Scriptures to us?"' When the penny had dropped, they learnt a very important lesson in recognising Jesus' presence.

Had Jesus revealed His identity immediately, they would have been so amazed by His resurrection that they wouldn't have taken in a word He had to say to them. Verse 27 says, 'And beginning with Moses and all the prophets He explained to them what was said in all the Scriptures concerning Himself.' You do not need to go to every conference or be at the centre of every sensational thing God is doing. Sometimes you are simply prevented from recognising Jesus. So, what do you do? Remain faithful and keep walking. If He isn't revealing His presence, that's okay, it just means you need to listen to what He is teaching you. You are no less valued in His sight; you just have a different assignment to carry out.

Prayer

Lord Jesus, I recognise that I am not to blame for 'missing it' and I don't have to be jealous of others or chase after signs and wonders. I commit to walking faithfully and listening to what You have to teach me along the way. Thank You for being closer than I could ever realise.

INSPIRE - Faith

DAY 27: DESPITE OTHER'S OPINIONS

While they were there, the time came for the baby to be born, and she gave birth to her firstborn, a son. She wrapped Him in cloths and placed Him in a manger, because there was no room for them in the inn. Luke 2:6-7

Context
'In those days Caesar Augustus issued a decree that a census should be taken of the entire Roman world' (v1). 'And everyone went to his own town to register' (v3). 'So, Joseph also went up from the town of Nazareth in Galilee to Judea, to Bethlehem the town of David, because he belonged to the house and line of David' (v4).

Today's Message
If I had to travel back to my home city of Leicester, where my family have lived for many years, naturally, I would stay with family. For one thing, I could catch up with family members I haven't seen in a while, and secondly, it's free accommodation! So, why didn't Joseph and Mary stay with Joseph's family? Take a moment to put these pieces of information together? 1. David's family was from Bethlehem, many of whom probably still lived there and 2. There was no room in the inn. Mary was pregnant out of wedlock. In the context of the deeply religious society of Judea at that time, this was a scandal! I highly suspect that Joseph's family had disassociated themselves from him and Mary. Leaving Joseph no choice but to unsuccessfully look for accommodation in inns, packed out by people arriving for the census.

Following God's plan isn't about making you popular. If it's fame you want, start a YouTube channel. Success in God's kingdom isn't defined by popularity. Mary had a choice, to say the baby was God's or lie and say she had slept with another man, either way she faced being stoned to death. Joseph also had a choice, to disgrace Mary or take her under his protection. As a righteous man he accepted the angel's message and chose the right way, despite facing criticism and rejection from others, sounding crazy and Joseph's family's disassociation. Yet they chose to obey the only One who's opinion mattered.

We are told soundbites in Christendom like "The best is yet to come". It's great for getting more out of volunteers, but this can leave people feeling ungrateful for what God has already done in their lives, as though salvation isn't enough. It also breeds unfulfillment like our purpose is forever just beyond our reach. But what if God has called you to live a seemingly normal life with no recognition attached, however, the result of your faithful life was so significant that the impact would be felt for the rest of history, would you do it? We only see snippets of Joseph's life, but what we do know is that he made the right choices, obeyed God, worked hard, and raised his children. All normal day to day stuff. But if he hadn't, what would have happened to Jesus and God's plan for all of humanity's salvation? You are called to be faithful. It may seem 'normal' but your life could be setting the stage for an incredible move of God in this and future generations.

Prayer
Lord God, I will be faithful in whatever You call me to do, whatever the cost. However normal life seems, I only want to please You.

DAY 28: THE OTHER SIDE

He called out to them, "Friends, haven't you any fish?" "No," they answered. He said, "Throw your net on the right side of the boat and you will find some." When they did, they were unable to haul the net in because of the large number of fish.
John 21:5-6

Context
Chapter 20:31 rounds off the gospel of John nicely with the words, 'But these are written that you may believe that Jesus is the Christ, the Son of God, and that by believing you may have life in His name.' However, John wasn't done, he records an incredible act of grace towards Peter in chapter 21. Peter not only had denied Jesus, but he had also returned to his default position of fisherman. Peter was referred to as Simon Peter in verse 3, was this an indication that his identity was in the balance? After about three and a half years of being on an amazing adventure with Jesus, it had all come to an end. Sports stars often experience a similar sense of emptiness and lack of purpose to life when their careers come to an end. What would Peter do with his life now? Peter returned to the only option that seemed available to him – fishing. After all, he was an expert in his field, or boat in this case. Certainly, writing an autobiography about his time with Jesus, and living off the proceeds wasn't really an option in those days.

Today's Message
Many of us have been doing church for a long time and are experts at it. But have we been merely pouring our efforts into looking and sounding like 'church,' but our nets have been on the wrong side of the boat all this time? Like Peter, we can look busy, even professional, we might go as far as calling it 'the Lord's work,' but is it what the Spirit is telling us to do? Lord, save us from our own efforts! No busyness, however good the intention, should ever replace a culture of miracles and salvation. Casting the net on the other side of the boat, naturally speaking, should not have made the slightest bit of difference. But obedience is the difference. Hearing what the Spirit is saying to the church is key to kingdom success, demonstrated by the simple catching of fish.

Notice that Jesus wasn't in the boat with Peter and the disciples. How many times have we gone off and done our own thing, just hoping that God would catch up with us and approve what we are doing? Jesus wasn't in their plans, but He was nearby. There are so many lessons we can learn from this passage (v1-14), but please take this one thought away with you today. You might look like you're doing all the right things for the right reasons, but is it what Jesus told you to do? He alone brings the supernatural element to a seemingly natural act, like changing sides of the boat. It may not make any logical sense, you may even get talked about, but the outcome will far exceed anything we could achieve in our efforts alone. Proverbs 3:5-6 says, 'Trust in the Lord with all your heart and lean not on your own understanding; in all your ways acknowledge Him, and He will make your paths straight.'

Prayer
Lord Jesus, I have often put my trust in my own understanding. Forgive me. What might seem logical, may not be the right thing to do. Like Peter, You haven't finished with me yet. Help me to 'cast my net' on the right side by listening and responding to Your Spirit.

DAY 29: HAVE A SERIOUS WORD WITH YOURSELF

Praise the LORD, O my soul; all my inmost being, praise His holy name. Praise the LORD, O my soul, and forget not all His benefits – who forgives all your sins and heals your diseases, who redeems your life from the pit and crowns you with love and compassion, who satisfies your desires with good things so that your youth is renewed like the eagle's. Psalm 103:1-5

Context

From time to time, we find ourselves in the fight for our lives, taking a battering from all sides or weighed down by the pressures of life. Sometimes it even feels like we must have a huge target pinned to our backs and if it could go wrong, it will. It is in these times, that the very first thing to go out of the window is praising God, followed by prayer and reading the Word. Then we isolate ourselves by withdrawing from our church family. But these choices only serve to make us more susceptible to further attacks from the enemy, with very little to protect ourselves with.

Today's Message

Every sports team receives a team talk or battle speech just before the game. But come half-time, if the team is losing, they get more than just a 'go get em' speech, they get a serious talking to.

A 'sort your life out' speech from the pulpit isn't going to gain the pastor much favour from the congregation, but sometimes that is exactly what we need. When life is hard and our heads drop, we need a talking to. Any army having just taken a pounding from a formidable enemy, needs to regroup and to hear a battle speech that will stir up courage and a determination to keep fighting.

If no one else is going to do it for you, you just need to have a serious word with yourself. Tell yourself that right now in the most difficult time, when everything seems hopeless, praise the Lord! Raise your own battle cry of praise. Otherwise, what are you speaking over yourself? Don't let negative and self-defeatist thoughts take control, they are lies from the enemy that seek to separate you from the Lord and His people.

Using the Psalms is a great place to start to stir your soul to praise. Tell yourself who our God is from His word. The Lord is not on an ego trip, He knows the benefits that praise has on our souls. Praise refocuses us to take our eyes off our circumstances and look to the Lord from whom our help comes. You might not feel like praising the Lord, it might even feel like it's the last thing you want to do, but praise is a powerful weapon, it's your battle cry that declares to the enemy who's side you are on, and that he has no authority or power in your life.

Prayer

Lord, You make Your ways known. You are compassionate and gracious, slow to anger abounding in love. You do not treat me as my sins deserve. For as high as the heavens are above the earth, so great is Your love for me who fear You. As far as the east is from the west, so far have You removed my sin from me. You have compassion on me like a father to a child. From everlasting to everlasting Your love is with me. You have established Your throne in heaven and Your kingdom rules over all. Praise the LORD, you His angels, you mighty ones who serve Him, who obey His word. Praise the LORD, all His heavenly hosts, you His servants who do His will. Praise the LORD, all His works everywhere in His dominion. Praise the LORD, O my soul. Psalm 103:7-22

DAY 30: CALLED BY MY NAME

If My people, who are called by My name, will humble themselves and pray and seek My face and turn from their wicked ways, then will I hear from heaven and will forgive their sin and will heal their land. **2 Chronicles 7:14**

Context

Solomon had just finished building the temple and royal palace. Fire from heaven had come down and consumed the offerings and the glory of the Lord filled the temple, to such an extent that the priests could not enter the temple. Then the Lord appeared at night and spoke to Solomon.

Today's Message

God calls us to 1. Humble ourselves, 2. Pray and seek God's face, and 3. Turn from our wicked ways. The Lord 1. WILL hear, 2. WILL forgive, and 3. WILL heal. It is the Lord's will to hear, forgive and heal. That is His heart's desire for His people, who are called by His name. This wasn't a mandate for a few, but every last one of the Lord's people. This calls for unity, to have a common purpose, putting aside differences and recognising our need to humble ourselves before our God. To acknowledge that we are totally dependent on Him, and that without Him we are hopelessly defenceless to the enemy and therefore, alone, we would be set to fail on an epic scale.

His Church, particularly in the western world, has spent far too long going through the motions of 'doing church', tolerating sin as 'being only human', celebrating showmanship as 'gifting' and endorsing division as 'different expressions'. This renders us powerless from operating in the power of the Spirit to the extent that we are promised in Scripture to all believers. We need to turn our backs on sin, and live in His forgiveness, presence and healing.

Many of us struggle to accept that all sin is the same in God's sight. How can a lie be as bad as murder, right? The actual act of sin isn't so much the issue, it's the damaging effect that sin has on us, our communities and more importantly on our relationship with God, that matters. All sin, no matter how small, separates us from God's holy presence both now on earth and for eternity in heaven. While we are compromising with sin, no amount of Christian slogans, out-of-context Bible verses on posters or charitable deeds will erase sin or usher in His presence. Only forgiveness through the blood of Jesus can remove sin and allow us to have a right relationship with Him.

Each one of us has a responsibility, not only for our own walk with Jesus, but to also hold each other accountable with love, to build up and encourage the Church and take responsibility for our nation's morality and corruption, in order to see the Lord's healing across our land. We, His people, called by His name are the gatekeepers to this happening. It starts with you and I. Together we must humble ourselves, pray and seek his face, with sincere repentance.

Prayer

Lord, this is a powerful verse, which requires a definite response from me. I'm so sorry for my sin, I lay it down. Sorry for my misplaced trust, I seek Your face and place my life into Your hands once again. Lord, hear my prayer, build Your Church and heal this land.

DAY 31: HEALTH CHECK

The fear of the LORD is the beginning of knowledge, but the fools despise wisdom and discipline. Proverbs 1: 7

The fear of the LORD is the beginning of wisdom; all who follow his precepts have good understanding. To Him belongs eternal praise. Psalm 111:10

Context

I hear Christians talk all the time about God's love, forgiveness, reconciliation and grace but that's only part of the gospel. I almost never hear anything about God's wrath and judgement or the fear of the Lord. The word fear has a very negative connotation to it but the fear of the Lord is different. The fear of the Lord is where true salvation starts. It's the moment we become conscious by the Holy Spirit, that we are a sinner and stand before the holy God, ashamed of our filthy sin, and know that without His forgiveness, we would have faced His wrath. God is so good, and He loves us, but He won't tolerate sin. He will not pardon sin, except through the blood of Jesus. The gospel is more than just love and forgiveness. We needed rescuing from sin and the Lord Himself rescued us from an eternity in hell, by enduring one of the most horrific deaths imaginable, as a sacrifice to pay for our costly sin. The debt was high, it cost everything, but Jesus made the payment and now the debt is paid. As a result, we want nothing more to do with sin.

Today's Message

Health check – do you fear the Lord? If not, why not? Matthew 10:28 says, 'do not be afraid of those who kill the body but cannot kill the soul. Rather, be afraid of the One who can destroy both soul and body in hell.' Proverbs 28:14 also says, 'Blessed is the man who always fears the Lord, but he who hardens his heart falls into trouble.' Conversely, to not fear the Lord, is to cast off His word as a fairy-tale and question whether you have ever surrendered your life to Him for salvation.

Why then do we play with sin and conveniently ignore the full gospel? The world doesn't need more lukewarm Christians only preaching the palatable parts of the gospel to entice and keep people in our churches. The problem is that much of the Church has grown fat on teaching and comfortable in complacency, distracted by fame and gimmicks. How can we change the world, if we look and sound just like the world?

The fear of the Lord ignites a passion that consumes us with love for Jesus and for those who don't yet know Him. The fear of the Lord will govern how we use our money, time and talents, our priorities, speech and behaviour. 'The LORD is my light and my salvation whom shall I fear? The LORD is the stronghold of my life – of whom shall I be afraid?' (Psalm 27:1). If we truly fear the Lord, we will not fear anything or anyone because our hope is secure in Him. Lets return to preaching the full gospel, which includes the judgement of God, then our churches would be filled with believers who have come to salvation on their knees under a conviction only possible through the Holy Spirit.

Prayer

Lord, my salvation cost You everything. May I never take it for granted, but always be grateful for what You have saved me from and to. Stir my heart, consume me with a passion for holiness and a hunger to see salvations from repentant hearts turning to You. To You belongs eternal praise.